Seahorses and Sea Dragons

TEXT BY MARY JO RHODES AND DAVID HALL
PHOTOGRAPHS BY DAVID HALL

Undersea Encounters

Children's Press
A Division of Scholastic Inc.
New York Toronto London Auckland Sydney
Mexico City New Delhi Hong Kong
Danbury, Connecticut

Library of Congress Cataloging-in-Publication Data

Rhodes, Mary Jo, 1957-
  Seahorses and sea dragons / Mary Jo Rhodes and David Hall; photographs by David Hall.
    p. cm. — (Undersea encounters)
  Includes bibliographical references (p.   ).
  ISBN 0-516-24393-4 (lib. bdg.)   0-516-25351-4 (pbk.)
  1. Sea horses—Juvenile literature. 2. Syngnathidae—Juvenile literature. I. Hall, David,
1943 Oct. 2- II. Title. III. Series.
  QL638.S9R48 2005
  597'.6798—dc22
                                    2004018915

*To my wife and dive buddy, Gayle Jamison. Without her support this project would not have
been possible.*
—D.H.
To my husband, John, and my sons Jeremy and Tim. This book is for them.
—M.J.R.

*Many thanks to Susan Newman for creating a beautiful sample book. Without her talent and
support this series might not have come to be.*

Photo credits:
All photographs © 2005 David Hall except: Corbis Images/Stephen Frink: 43; Rudie
Kuiter: 36, 37, 39 inset; Seapics.com/Ingrid Visser: 42.

Leafy sea dragons take camouflage to the extreme !
pg. 26

Pygmy seahorses are actually the size of your fingernail.
pg. 29

Seahorses and Sea Dragons

Male seahorses give birth to their own babies!
pg. 35

A pot-bellied seahorse clings to a giant kelp plant.

chapter 1

What Is a Seahorse?

Imagine a creature with the head of a horse and the tail of a monkey. This creature is almost invisible to its enemies. It sucks in food like a vacuum cleaner. It also grows plants on its back.

The creature you have just imagined is a real animal called a seahorse. A seahorse is a fish. Like other fish, a seahorse lives in water and breathes with **gills**. It also has fins and a backbone.

Seahorse Names

Scientists use two names to identify all living things: a genus (JEE-nus) name and a species (SPEE-sees) name. The genus name for all seahorses is *Hippocampus*. In Greek, *Hippos* means "horse," and *kampos* means "sea monster."

Each kind of seahorse has its own species name. The scientific name for this painted seahorse is *Hippocampus sindonis*. This means "woven cloth" in Latin.

Seahorses are different from other fish in some ways, too. Most fish are covered with scales. Scales are hard plates that protect the body. Seahorses don't have scales. Instead, they have tough skin that covers an outer skeleton. The skeleton is made up of bony plates and rings.

Size of a Seahorse

Seahorses come in different sizes. A pygmy seahorse can be as small as a fly. A pot-bellied seahorse is about the size of a robin. Most seahorses are about 4 to 6 inches (10 to 15 centimeters) long, from the coronet, or knob on top of their heads, to the tips of their tails.

Fish Fact

There may be more than fifty species of seahorses. Some seahorses are still waiting for scientists to give them a name!

Seahorse Relatives

Seahorses are part of a family of fish called **Syngnathidae** (sin-NATH-ih-DEE). The other members of this family are sea dragons, pipefishes, and pipehorses. Syngnathidae means "fused jaws" in Greek. All of these animals have jaws that are joined together, or fused, to form a long snout.

Sea Dragons

Sea dragons are some of the strangest looking fish in the sea. Skin growths that look like branching seaweed sprout from their bodies. Sea dragons are larger than seahorses. Adults are 18 inches (45 cm) long, about the length of a crow.

Pipefishes

A pipefish looks like a seahorse that has been stretched out. It is long and thin, like a pencil. Pipefishes may be up to 2 feet (60 cm) long. Scientists have named more than two hundred species of pipefishes.

Pipehorses

Pipehorses appear to be part seahorse and part pipefish. They have curling tails like seahorses. But, like pipefishes, their heads are in more of a straight line with their bodies.

Seahorses have a strong tail
for holding on to seaweed, coral,
and other stationary objects.

chapter 2

Where Do Seahorses Live?

Walking along a beach, you might be surprised to learn that seahorses and their relatives are living nearby. Seahorses don't swim far out into the open sea. They like to stay in shallow water, near the shore.

The ideal seahorse **habitat** has lots of things that seahorses can wrap their tails around. Seahorses also need to have a steady current of water. This current helps bring **prey** close enough to be sucked in easily.

The short-headed seahorse is found only in Australia.

Seahorses are marine animals. This means they live in salt water. They are found in oceans all around the world. Most species are found in the warm, tropical waters of the Indian and Pacific oceans. More than twenty-five seahorse species are found around the coastline of Australia alone.

Undersea Gardens and Meadows

In tropical seas, seahorses might be found in places with soft coral or in sponge gardens. Many seahorses and pipefishes live in or near seagrass beds. These are underwater meadows found in muddy or sandy areas.

Coral reefs provide homes for one-quarter of all marine plants and animals, including many seahorses and pipefishes.

Seagrass beds are an important habitat for many ocean animals, including sea-horses.

Fish Fact

Seahorses don't travel far. Most male seahorses have a **home range** about the size of a desk. Female seahorses roam a larger area, about the size of a classroom.

Undersea Forests

In cooler water, seahorses and sea dragons sometimes live in underwater "forests" of kelp. Kelp is a type of seaweed. Sea dragons live only in kelp forests along the southern coast of Australia.

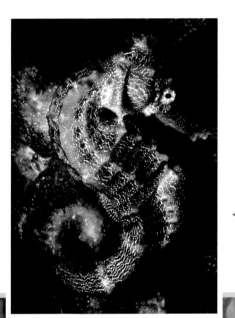

A few seahorse species live along the coasts of North America. The lined, dwarf, and longsnout seahorses live along the East Coast. The Pacific seahorse is found along the West Coast.

◄ The Pacific seahorse is found along the West Coast, from South America to California.

A weedy sea dragon swims through an underwater "forest" of giant kelp.

A Fish With a Monkey's Tail

The long tail of a seahorse is made for holding on to things. A seahorse may wrap its strong tail around any nearby object, such as a branch of seaweed or coral. This protects the animal from being swept away from its home by powerful ocean waves or currents. Seahorses and pipehorses are the only fish that have this unusual tail.

Unlike a seahorse, the leafy sea dragon swims through the water head-first.

chapter 3

Seahorses on the Move

Imagine trying to swim while wearing a suit of armor. You might not be able to bend or move very freely. The bodies of seahorses and sea dragons are covered with a kind of bony armor. A fish cannot swim fast if it can't bend its body easily.

There are also other reasons why seahorses and sea dragons are slow swimmers. Most other fish get extra swimming power from their large tail fins. When a fish swims, the tail

Unlike seahorses, barracudas are built for speed. They have a long, thin shape, a flexible body, and a large tail fin.

fin whips from side to side. This movement helps to push the fish through the water.

Seahorses are different. They swim in an upright position. They also have a pointed tail with no fin on the end. Their tails are good for holding on to things, but not for swimming.

Fish Fact

Seahorses are among the slowest fish in the ocean. It would take some seahorses more than an hour to cross a swimming pool.

Hidden Fins

Seahorses and sea dragons have fins that are so thin you can see right through them. The dorsal fin is located on the animal's back. It beats rapidly and pushes the seahorse or sea dragon forward slowly. When the animal is not swimming, its fins are folded tightly against its body and are difficult to see.

A pair of pectoral fins stick out from the sides of a seahorse's or sea dragon's head. These fins help the animal to balance and steer. Because their fins

Seahorses and sea dragons use their dorsal fin to push them through the water. Their pectoral fins help them steer.

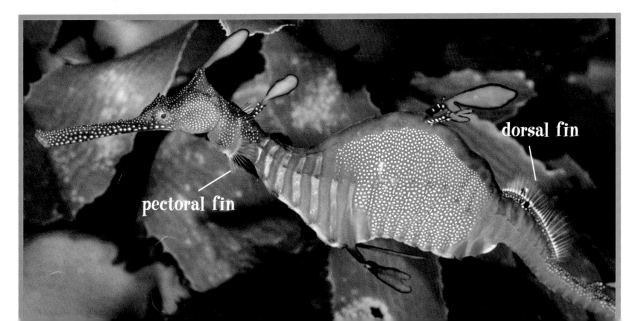

pectoral fin

dorsal fin

are almost invisible, seahorses and sea dragons appear to swim as if by magic.

Seahorses may be slow, but they are skilled swimmers. They can move backward and forward. They can steer with great control. They can also turn easily around a single blade of grass. Seahorses will even ride an underwater current to get someplace more quickly.

A seahorse's pointy tail is good for holding on to things, but is not much use when it comes to swimming.

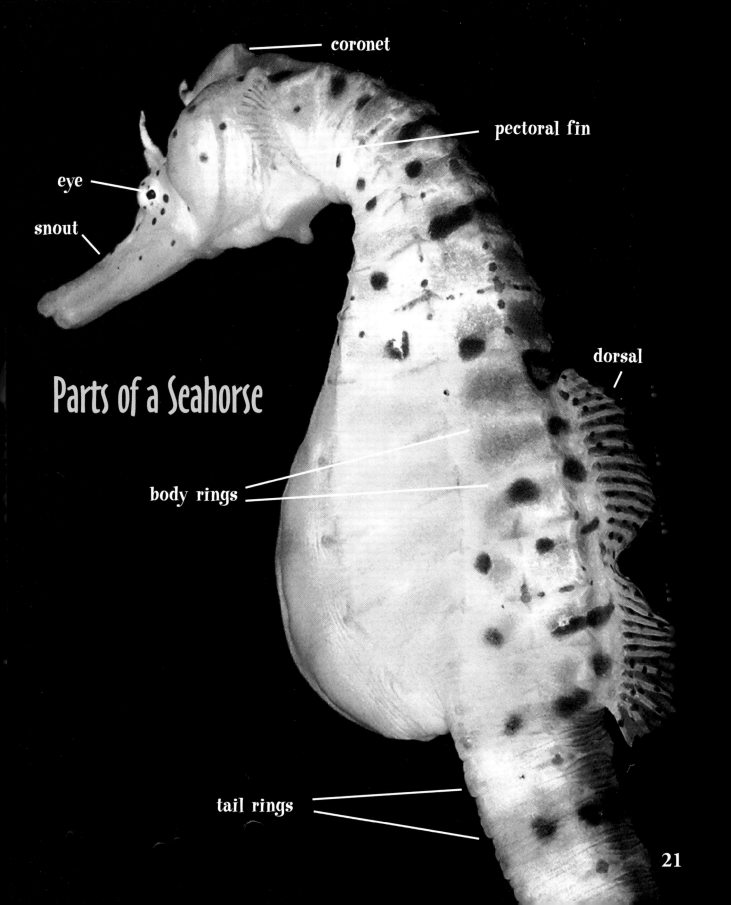

coronet

pectoral fin

eye

snout

dorsal

Parts of a Seahorse

body rings

tail rings

21

This dark seahorse has algae that looks like hair growing on its skin. White grains of sand have become stuck in the algae, helping to disguise the seahorse.

chapter 4

The Invisible Seahorse

If you were to go snorkeling or scuba diving where seahorses live, you would probably have a hard time finding one. Seahorses are experts at making themselves almost invisible.

Seahorses can change their skin color to match their surroundings. This is a form of **camouflage**. They may become brown to blend in with mangrove roots. Or they might turn yellowish green like seaweed. Others may become orange or red like a nearby sponge.

Seahorses are able to change color because of special **cells** in their skin. These cells contain tiny sacs of color **pigment**. Different mixtures of these pigments can make many color shades and patterns.

The longsnout seahorse has an amazing ability to change color. It is able to blend in with almost any surroundings. (Left with a red sponge; bottom with pale algae; right with yellow coral.)

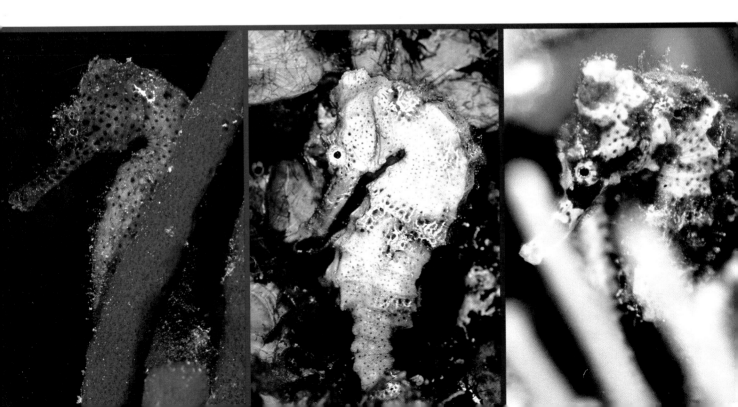

Plant or Animal?

Seahorses also have other ways to camouflage themselves. Some seahorses grow long strands of skin that look like branching seaweed.

A pot-bellied seahorse can grow long strands of skin to hide among seaweed branches.

Other seahorses have tiny plants called **algae** (AL-gee) growing on their skin. This gives them a fuzzy appearance and helps them to hide from predators.

The behavior of leafy sea dragons adds to their camouflage shape and color. They usually sway back and forth with the ocean waves, just like the nearby seaweeds. When a predator comes close, a sea dragon will turn and face away. This makes the animal even harder to recognize.

The leafy sea dragon is one of the most perfectly camouflaged fish in the sea.

Pipefishes and pipehorses are also masters of camouflage. The double-ended pipehorse looks just like a blade of seagrass. Only its eyes reveal that it is an animal and not a plant.

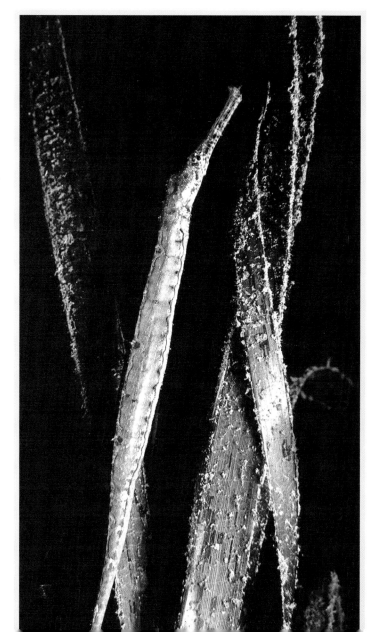

A double-ended pipehorse hides among nearby blades of seagrass. This is another example of camouflage.

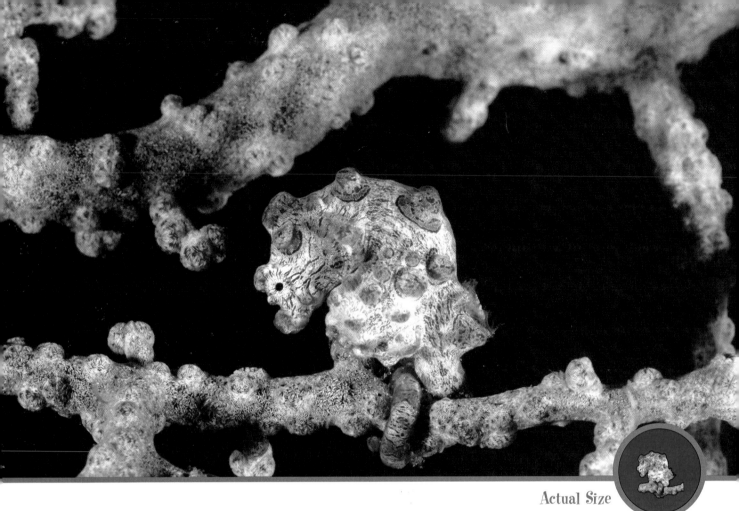

Actual Size

Pygmy Seahorses

Bargibant's Pygmy Seahorse

You need sharp eyes to find **pygmy** seahorses. They were unknown until around 1970, when a scientist named Georges Bargibant found one. It was clinging to a piece of branching coral that he had collected for a museum. The seahorse, *Hippocampus bargibanti*, was named for him.

A Bargibant's pygmy seahorse measures almost 1 inch (25 millimeters) with its tail stretched out. It has pink, wart-like growths on its skin. These growths help the seahorse to hide among the coral it lives on.

28

Denise's Pygmy Seahorse

More pygmy seahorses have been discovered recently. Denise's pygmy seahorse is even smaller than Bargibant's. About the size of your fingernail, it is one of the tiniest fish in the sea.

Actual Size

This leafy sea dragon is swimming with tiny mysids, its favorite prey.

chapter 5

Predator and Prey

Seahorses and sea dragons are **predators**. They suck in prey through their long snouts. They don't have teeth or movable jaws, so they must swallow their prey whole.

Seahorses and sea dragons feed on **zooplankton** (zo-uh-PLANK-tun). These are very small animals that drift with the ocean currents.

Among their favorite foods are **mysids**. A mysid is a tiny animal that looks a bit like a shrimp, but is smaller than a mosquito. A hungry seahorse or

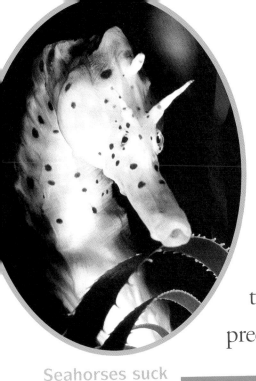

sea dragon may eat more than a thousand mysids in one day!

Seahorses as Prey

Seahorses may also become prey. But they are usually very well hidden. Most predators swim by without noticing them.

Seahorses suck in prey through a small opening at the end of their snout.

A weedy sea dragon goes unnoticed by this large fish.

Also, their bony bodies are not a tasty meal for most animals.

But seahorses, especially young ones, are eaten by some animals. Both seahorses and pipefishes have been found in the stomachs of flounders and other bottom-dwelling fish.

A flounder has captured a stick pipefish. You can still see the pipefish's tail sticking out of the flounder's mouth.

Fish Fact

A seahorse can move each eye separately. It can watch for predators with one eye and look for prey with the other.

This male seahorse has a bulging brood pouch, which means that he is pregnant.

chapter 6

Fathers That Give Birth

Can a father also be a mother? The answer is "yes" if the father is a seahorse. This may sound strange. Usually, only female animals give birth. But seahorses and sea dragons are different. It is the male, not the female, who gives birth to their young!

A Seahorse "Couple"

The male and the female seahorse greet one another every day at the same time. They may twirl around a blade of grass or swim together side

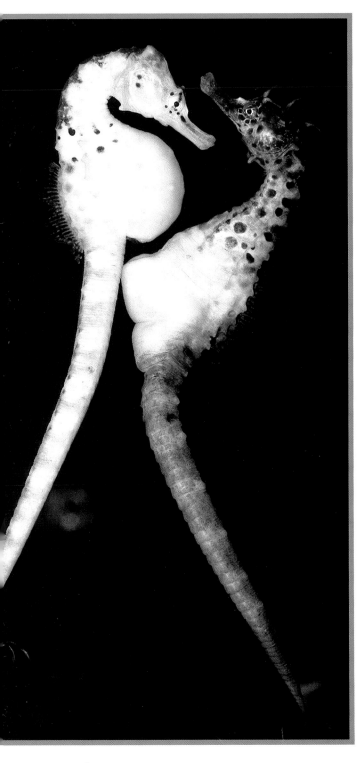

by side for a while. This creates a strong bond between the seahorses.

A few days later the male's **brood pouch**, a small sac on the front of his body, fills with water. He pushes the water out, causing his pouch to open wide. The female can see that he is ready for her eggs. The pair then come together as the female directs her eggs into the male's pouch.

The female seahorse (on the left) is about to place her eggs into the male's pouch.

Inside the Pouch

Once the eggs are safely inside, the pouch seals shut. The eggs are then fertilized by the male's **sperm**. A male pygmy seahorse may carry as few as five eggs in his tiny pouch. Larger male seahorses can hold several hundred eggs.

Male seahorses carry and protect the eggs for several weeks. During this time, a baby seahorse develops and grows inside each egg.

This male White's seahorse is giving birth to dozens of babies, one or two at a time.

A Seahorse Is Born

When the seahorses are fully developed, they will hatch out of eggs while still inside the pouch. The babies then get pushed out one or two at a time.

After they are born, baby seahorses are on their own. At first, they may drift with the ocean currents. After a few weeks, they settle down on the sea bottom. Many young seahorses are eaten by other fish. In some cases, only one or two out of a thousand babies may survive to become adults.

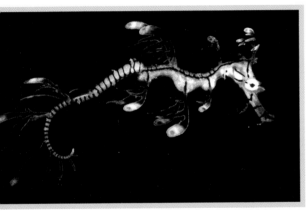

This leafy sea dragon is just a few days old.

Fish Fact

Small seahorses live for about a year. Larger seahorses live for an average of three to five years.

This is a pregnant male leafy sea dragon with pink eggs under his tail.

Sea Dragon Fathers

A male sea dragon does not have a brood pouch. Instead, he has special skin underneath his tail called a brood "patch." The female dragon attaches her eggs there and the male fertilizes them. He carries the eggs under his tail for several weeks until they hatch.

(Above) Baby leafy sea dragons are hatching. The young sea dragons come out of the eggs tail-first.

A scuba diver watches a leafy sea dragon. Sea dragons are protected by law in Australia.

chapter 7

Seahorses, Sea Dragons, and People

Seahorses and sea dragons have lived in the ocean for millions of years. They have adapted to many changes in their surroundings. But, like other sea animals, they face problems caused by humans.

Seahorses in Danger

Some people in Asia and other parts of the world believe that seahorses are useful in treating health problems.

Millions of seahorses are caught each year and are ground up into powder for making medicines. Dried seahorses are also sometimes made into jewelry and other objects sold in stores.

People may do things that harm seahorses without even knowing it. For example, we can hurt seahorses and other ocean animals by destroying or polluting the places where they live. Waste products from farms and factories may be washed into the sea and damage their habitats.

Dried seahorses and pipehorses are for sale in an outdoor market.

Protecting Seahorses

Many wildlife organizations are working hard to protect seahorses. All seahorse species are now protected by an agreement that has been signed by more than 160 countries. The buying and selling of seahorses is watched closely to make sure that too many are not removed from the wild.

Seahorses are sometimes kept as pets. But they are picky eaters and often get sick when kept in home aquariums. Most will not survive as pets for more than a few weeks.

If you want to see live seahorses, sea dragons, and pipefishes, you can visit a public aquarium. Many aquariums have special seahorse exhibits. Some aquariums also breed seahorses, so that fewer need to be collected from the wild.

Seahorses and sea dragons are special animals, but we need to protect them and their habitats. If we capture too many or destroy their habitats, there will be fewer left for everyone to enjoy.

A scuba diver comes face to face with a longsnout seahorse.

Glossary

algae (**AL-jee**) simple plants that are common in the ocean. Seaweed is a kind of algae. *(pg. 26)*

brood pouch (**brood pouch**) an expandable sac on the front of a male seahorse in which he carries fertilized eggs until they have hatched. *(pg. 36)*

camouflage (**KAM-uh-flahzh**) the ability of an animal to blend in with its surroundings to become nearly invisible. *(pg. 23)*

cells (**sels**) tiny "building blocks" of all living things; the basic structural units of all plants and animals. *(pg. 24)*

genus (**JEE-nuhss**) a group of very closely related animals. All seahorses belong to the genus *Hippocampus*. *(pg. 6)*

gills (**gils**) organs that fish use to breathe. Gills absorb oxygen dissolved in the surrounding water. *(pg. 5)*

habitat (**HAB-uh-tat**) any place where plants and animals live. *(pg. 11)*

home range (**home raynj**) the geographic area in which an animal carries out its normal activities. *(pg. 13)*

mysid (**MYE-sid**) tiny swimming animals related to shrimps. Mysids are a favorite food for sea dragons and many seahorses. *(pg. 31)*

pigment (**PIG-muhnt**) a natural substance in a plant or animal that gives it color. (*pg. 24*)

predator (**PRED-uh-tur**) an animal that hunts and kills other animals for food. (*pg. 31*)

prey (**pray**) an animal that is killed and eaten by another animal. (*pg. 12*)

pygmy (**PIG-mee**) an especially small kind of animal. (*pg. 28*)

species (**SPEE-sheez**) a particular kind of animal or plant. All members of a single species have a very similar appearance and genetic makeup. (*pg. 6*)

sperm (**spurm**) the cells produced by a male animal that can fertilize the eggs produced by a female. An egg must be fertilized before it can grow and develop into a baby animal. (*pg. 37*)

Syngnathidae (**sin-NATH-ih-DEE**) the animal family to which seahorses, pipefishes, and sea dragons belong. These animals are called syngnathids. (*pg. 8*)

zooplankton (**ZO-uh-PLANK-tun**) small, microscopic animals that drift in currents. (*pg. 31*)

Learn More About Seahorses and Sea Dragons

Book

Walker, Sally M. *Sea Horses*. Minneapolis: Carolrhoda Books, Inc., 1999.

Magazines

Hall, David, "Dragons of the Sea," *Ocean Realm*, Summer 1997.

Vincent, Amanda, "The Improbable Seahorse," *National Geographic*, October 1994.

Web Sites

Kingdom of the Seahorse, Nova Online (www.pbs.org/wgbh/nova/seahorse/)

Saving Seahorses, Monterey Bay Aquarium, Monterey, California (www.sheddaquarium.org/exh_seahorse.htm)

Seahorse Symphony, Shedd Aquarium, Chicago, Illinois (www.sheddaquarium.org/exh_seahorse.html)

Seahorse Surreal, Oregon Coast Aquarium, Newport, Oregon (www.aquarium.org/education/spotlight/seahorses/)

Secrets of the Seahorse, Birch Aquarium, La Jolla, California (aquarium.ucsd.edu/new_site/)

Organizations

Project Seahorse (seahorse.fisheries.ubc.ca)

Dragon Search (Sea Dragons) (www.dragonsearch.asn.au/)

Index

About the Authors

After earning degrees in zoology and medicine, **David Hall** has worked for the past twenty-five years as both a wildlife photojournalist and a physician. David's articles and photographs have appeared in hundreds of calendars, books, and magazines, including *National Geographic, Smithsonian, Natural History*, and *Ranger Rick*. His underwater images have won many major awards including *Nature's Best*, BBC Wildlife Photographer of the Year, and Festival Mondial de l'Image Sous-Marine.

Mary Jo Rhodes became interested in seahorses through her involvement with Project Seahorse, a conservation organization.

She received her M.S. in Library Service from Columbia University and was a librarian for the Brooklyn Public Library. She later worked for ten years in children's book publishing in New York City.

Mary Jo lives with her husband, John Rounds, and two teenage sons, Jeremy and Tim, in Hoboken, New Jersey.

About the Consultant

Acknowledged as one of the world's foremost seahorse and sea dragon experts, **Rudie Kuiter** is a research associate in the zoology department of the Museum of Victoria, Australia, and an associate in the ichthyology section of the Australian Museum. He is the author of more than thirty scientific papers and many books about marine life, including *Seahorses, Pipefishes and Their Relatives*.